HOCKEY'S ORIGIN STORY

by Robb Murray

CAPSTONE PRESS
a capstone imprint

Published by Capstone Press, an imprint of Capstone
1710 Roe Crest Drive, North Mankato, Minnesota 56003
capstonepub.com

Copyright © 2025 by Capstone. All rights reserved. No part of this publication may
be reproduced in whole or in part, or stored in a retrieval system, or transmitted
in any form or by any means, electronic, mechanical, photocopying, recording, or
otherwise, without written permission of the publisher.

SPORTS ILLUSTRATED KIDS is a trademark of ABG-SI LLC.
Used with permission.

Library of Congress Cataloging-in-Publication Data is available
on the Library of Congress website
ISBN: 9781669090168 (hardcover)
ISBN: 9781669090113 (paperback)
ISBN: 9781669090120 (ebook PDF)

Summary: Follow the sport of hockey from its early days until today.
Learn how the sport has changed along the way and who has changed it.

Editorial Credits
Editor: Mandy Robbins; Designer: Elyse White; Media Researcher: Jo Miller;
Production Specialist: Tori Abraham

Image Credits
Alamy: Cal Sport Media, 19, History and Art Collection, 8, Pictures Now, 12,
ZUMA Press, Inc., 18, 20, 26; Bridgeman Images: David Lees Photography Archive,
6; Getty Images: andreygonchar, 15, Bruce Bennett, 27, Focus On Sport, 21,
Grafissimo, cover (bottom), 5, Icon Sportswire, 11, 28, Popperfoto, 13, Science &
Society Picture Library, 7, Scott Halleran, 25, The Asahi Shimbun, 24; Shutterstock:
photographer2222, cover (top), Sergey Novikov, 23; Sports Illustrated: David E.
Klutho , 16, Manny Millan, 17, Neil Leifer, 14

Any additional websites and resources referenced in this book are not maintained,
authorized, or sponsored by Capstone. All product and company names are
trademarks™ or registered® trademarks of their respective holders.

Printed and bound in China. 6098

TABLE OF CONTENTS

INTRODUCTION
THE FIRST OFFICIAL HOCKEY GAME 4

CHAPTER 1
EARLY ORIGINS 6

CHAPTER 2
CHANGES TO THE GAME 10

CHAPTER 3
TOP PLAYERS AND THE TOP AWARD 16

CHAPTER 4
A GAME FOR EVERYONE 22

Timeline	29
Glossary	30
Read More	31
Internet Sites	31
Index	32
About the Author	32

Words in **bold** are in the glossary.

INTRODUCTION
THE FIRST OFFICIAL HOCKEY GAME

If you could travel back in time to see the first organized hockey game, you would find yourself in Montreal, Canada. The date was March 3, 1875. This game saw the first-ever use of a puck. Previously, games had been played on frozen lakes, rivers, and ponds using a ball. But on this day, players made a chunk of wood into a disc. This new puck offered more control than a ball.

Over the next 150 years, hockey's rules and equipment have **evolved**. And the sport has become more welcoming to all. The result is a game that millions of people have grown to love.

A hockey game on a frozen lake in the 1890s

CHAPTER 1
EARLY ORIGINS

Who invented hockey? There is no clear answer to the question. Some people trace it back to games played in ancient Greece and Egypt with a stick and ball. Some say it was invented in Ethiopia in 1000 **BCE** or Iran in 2000 BCE. The first clues we have about a game played on a frozen surface come from Scotland. It was in the early 1600s, and it was called shinty.

An engraving of young men playing a stick-and-ball game in Greece in 510 BCE

Young men of the Araucano nation in present-day Chile played a version of hockey.

Around the same time in England, people played a similar game called bandy. Its players soon began using iron skates. British soldiers brought the game across the Atlantic Ocean to eastern Canada. But Native peoples there were already playing a similar game too, which looked like lacrosse. However it was invented, hockey's popularity grew fast.

FOUNDING FIGURES

As the game of hockey evolved, Canadians led the way in creating its rules. One of them was James G. A. Creighton. He attended the first game and helped form the first rules. He **recruited** players from nearby McGill University in Montreal.

A hockey game at McGill University in 1884

Another founding figure was Lady Isobel Gathorne-Hardy. She was an avid fan of the game and enjoyed playing, herself. In 1890, she played in one of the first organized hockey games for women in Québec at just 15 years old. She later helped convince her father, Lord Stanley, to donate a cup to award to the best **amateur** team in North American. Today the Stanley Cup is awarded to the winner of the National Hockey League (NHL) playoffs.

The Patrick family is also legendary in Canada. Brothers Lester and Frank Patrick introduced new rules and tactics to the game as players and managers. They included the forward pass, the playoff system, and **penalty** shots. Their father, Joe Patrick, paid for the construction of Canada's first indoor ice arenas in British Columbia. In 1911, the Patricks even started their own hockey league—the Pacific Coast Hockey Association.

CHAPTER 2
CHANGES TO THE GAME

Much has changed in the sport of hockey since it began. Not least of all is the game's setting. The only playing surface ice hockey can be played on is, of course, ice. Early players found ice in nature. Native peoples, including those from the Navajo and Cherokee nations, played a game called shinny hockey. They played on frozen ponds and lakes. There were no rules about the size of the playing surface. In bandy, rules called for an ice surface as large as a football field!

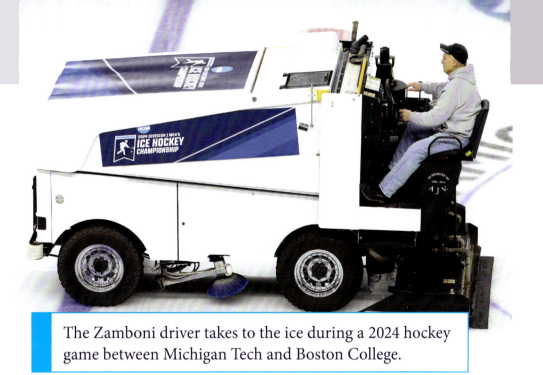

The Zamboni driver takes to the ice during a 2024 hockey game between Michigan Tech and Boston College.

Most modern hockey rinks come in two sizes. NHL rinks are 200 feet (61 meters) long and 85 feet (26 m) wide. Olympic-sized rinks are slightly larger. They are 200 feet (61 m) by 100 feet (30.5 m). No matter the size of the rink, a **Zamboni** is required to clean up the ice and make it fresh.

FACT

A brand-new Zamboni, which cleans and adds fresh water to smooth rink surfaces, can cost up to $250,000. Its top speed is 9 miles (14.5 kilometers) per hour.

11

CHANGING RULES

Early versions of hockey were played by rules not found in today's game. The number of skaters allowed on the ice dropped from nine to seven to five. Games consisted of two 30-minute halves rather than three 20-minute periods.

Years ago, goalies had to remain standing at all times. That changed in 1917, when the NHL removed the rule. Now goalies can do whatever they need to do to stop the puck.

Officials added the "no icing" rule in 1937. Icing is when a team flings the puck to the other end of the rink to relieve pressure on the goalie.

Outdoor ice hockey, 1901

An international game between Canada and Germany in the 1930s

FACT

The biggest blowout in NHL history occurred on January 23, 1944. The Detroit Red Wings beat the New York Rangers 15–0.

PROTECTIVE GEAR

It's hard to believe now, but hockey players once didn't wear helmets. That changed in 1979, when the NHL required all incoming players to wear them. By 1983, the helmet rule applied to all.

In the early days, players weren't required to wear any protective gear. Many chose to use leather or wood to protect their shins. Players today wear pads to protect their shins, shoulders, and elbows.

Montreal Canadiens goalie Lorne "Gump" Worsley 1966

Modern hockey skates

Skates are an important piece of hockey gear. Early players strapped removable blades onto leather boots. Today, specialized hockey skates are often a player's most expensive piece of equipment.

No player needs protection more than goaltenders. In the early years, felt pads were their main source of protection. Today, goalies wear thick gloves for catching and blocking pucks. Leg pads provide a wall of protection from the knees down. And special masks protect their faces from flying pucks.

CHAPTER 3
TOP PLAYERS AND THE TOP AWARD

Any discussion of the greatest players of all time must include Gordie Howe, Mario Lemieux, and Wayne Gretzky. Howe was the oldest player to play in NHL history, retiring at age 52. He is also fourth in all-time scoring with 1,850 points. Lemieux had unmatched grit and drive. He scored on his first-ever shift. Lemieux put his career on hold at age 27, when he announced that he had cancer. After two months of treatment, he scored in his first game back.

Mario Lemieux

Wayne Gretzky is nicknamed The Great One. His career rewrote the record books. To this day he still holds nearly every major scoring record, including the single-season points record of 215.

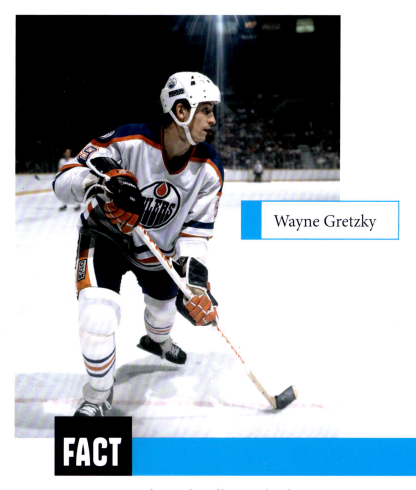

Wayne Gretzky

FACT

Wayne Gretzky is the all-time highest scorer in professional hockey. His 2,857 points give him more than a 900-point lead over the competition.

17

THE NEW GENERATION

Through the 2023–24 season, Connor McDavid has played nine seasons with the Edmonton Oilers. At that time, he had notched nearly 1,000 points.

Connor Bedard of the Chicago Blackhawks is one of the NHL's flashiest young stars. He went pro in 2023 when he was just 18 years old. He was a top-three finalist for the 2024 Calder Trophy, awarded to the **Rookie** of the Year.

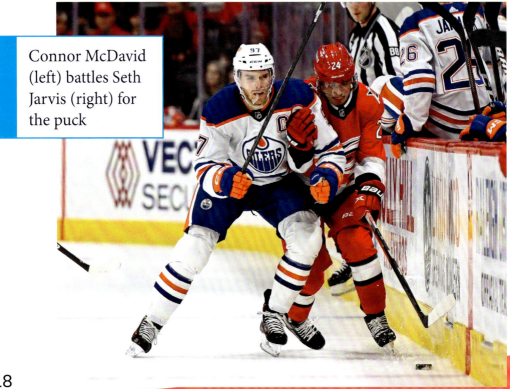

Connor McDavid (left) battles Seth Jarvis (right) for the puck

Hillary Knight is a force in women's hockey. She's played for several U.S. National and Olympic teams. In 2023, she was named the International Ice Hockey Federation Female Player of the Year.

In 2023, Laila Edwards became the first Black woman on the U.S. National Team. A standout player for the Wisconsin Badgers, Edwards helped her college team win a national title.

Laila Edwards

THE STANLEY CUP

The Stanley Cup is the oldest trophy in North America. It was donated in 1892 by Sir Frederick Arthur Stanley. There are actually three Stanley Cups. One is the original, which was donated by Lord Stanley. The second is the "presentation cup." It is presented to the winning NHL team each season. The third is a **replica** that is displayed at the Hockey Hall of Fame.

The Montreal Canadiens have won the most Stanley Cup championships with 24! Each time a team wins the cup, the names of each player are **etched** onto the trophy.

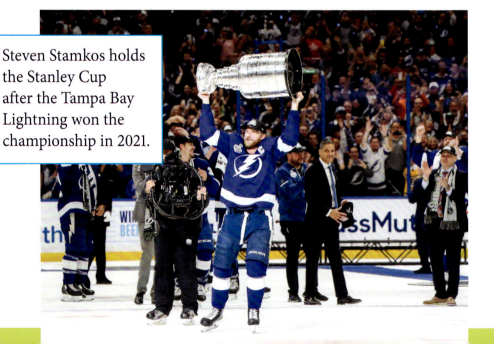

Steven Stamkos holds the Stanley Cup after the Tampa Bay Lightning won the championship in 2021.

Starting in 1995, the NHL gave each player from the winning team 24 hours with the Stanley Cup. Players have had their babies baptized in it. A few took it swimming. And many have used the cup for a cereal bowl!

MIRACLE ON ICE

The 1980 "Miracle on Ice" is one of the most famous games in hockey history. The U.S. Men's National Team faced the Soviet Union in the Olympic semifinals. The Soviets were four-time defending champs and highly favored to win again. Herb Brooks was Team USA's head coach. He inspired his crew of all college players to upset the Soviets 4–3. Team USA went on to win the gold!

CHAPTER 4
A GAME FOR EVERYONE

Hockey isn't just a game for professional athletes. Amateur hockey has thrived since the early days of the sport. There are more than 500,000 youth hockey players in the United States today. In Canada, more than 600,000 youth players are registered for hockey.

Hobey Baker was one of the greatest amateur players ever. In the early 1900s, he used speed and stickhandling to weave through defenses. And he always shook hands with opposing teams after games. Baker's skill and sportsmanship are remembered today. The award for the top male college hockey player each year is called the Hobey Baker Award.

There was a time when most NHL players came from Canada and the United States. But in recent years, players from other countries have made their mark. They include Alex Ovechkin from Russia and Jaromir Jagr from the Czech Republic.

A youth hockey team poses for an intimidating photo.

WOMEN'S CHAMPIONSHIPS

In the early 1900s, women's leagues sprouted up in New York and Boston. In 1964, the first women's college hockey team was formed at Brown University.

Women's hockey became an Olympic sport at the 1998 Winter Games in Nagano, Japan. That year, Team USA beat Canada in a thrilling gold-medal game. That win led to a boom in U.S. girls youth hockey. According to the magazine *USA Hockey*, participation in girls' hockey increased 65 percent from 2008 to 2023.

Team USA's Sarah Tueting, makes a save during the 1998 Winter Olympics championship game.

Similar growth has been seen in the college ranks. After Brown launched the first women's team, several other schools followed. But it wasn't until 2000 that the National Collegiate Athletic Association (NCAA) began overseeing women's college hockey. Today, more than 100 U.S. colleges and universities have women's hockey programs.

MANON RHÉAUME: "THE FIRST WOMAN OF HOCKEY"

Manon Rhéaume made history in 1992. She became the first woman to play in an NHL game. She's still the only woman to have ever done so.

Rhéaume suited up as a goaltender for two preseason games for the Tampa Bay Lightning. She also played for a number of men's minor league teams. Rhéaume was also part of the silver medal–winning Canadian women's hockey team in the 1998 Winter Olympics.

PROFESSIONAL WOMEN'S HOCKEY

The Professional Women's Hockey League (PWHL) began play in 2024 with six teams. The first game was played in front of a packed stadium in Toronto. Nearly 3 million people watched on television as New York beat Toronto 4–0.

The PWHL wasn't the first attempt at a women's league. The Premier Hockey Federation ran from 2015 to 2023. The league ended when it was purchased by the PWHL.

Liz Schepers takes a shot during a PWHL game.

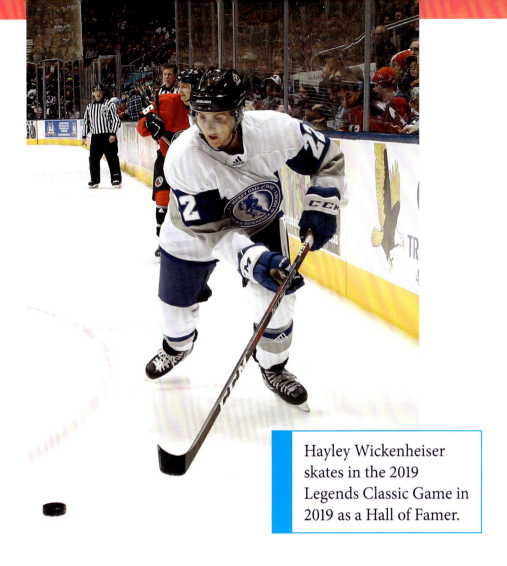

Hayley Wickenheiser skates in the 2019 Legends Classic Game in 2019 as a Hall of Famer.

The women's game has had its share of superstars. Cammi Granato captained the U.S. women's team that won Olympic gold in 1998. Natalie Darwitz collected three Olympic medals during her playing career. Canada's Hayley Wickenheiser was the first woman to score a goal in a professional men's game.

A GROWING SPORT

Hockey's popularity is still growing. The NHL is adding new teams, and the PWHL is drawing new fans to the game. Leagues in Europe and Asia are drawing even more fan attention as well.

Hockey used to be a game played only in cold climates. But in the last 30 years, it has reached into the southern United States. There are professional teams in Texas, Florida, California, and Nevada. The sport that was once played on frozen ponds and rivers is now played in stadiums packed with screaming fans.

TIMELINE

1875 The first organized hockey game is played in Montreal.

1890 The first women's hockey game is held.

1892 Sir Frederick Arthur Stanley donates the Stanley Cup.

1949 Frank Zamboni invents an ice-resurfacing machine.

1979 All incoming NHL players are required to wear helmets.

1980 The U.S. Men's Hockey team upsets the Soviets in the Miracle on Ice.

1981 The Hobey Baker Award is established.

1983 All NHL players are required to wear helmets.

2004-5 The NHL season was shut down due to a dispute between players and owners.

2008 The Kontinental Hockey League (KHL) was established.

2015 The Premier Hockey Federation begins as a professional women's league.

2024 The Professional Women's Hockey League takes over the Premier Hockey Federation.

GLOSSARY

amateur (AM-uh-chur)—describes a sports league that athletes take part in for pleasure rather than for money

BCE (bee-see-EE)—before the Common Era; it begins by counting backward at the year zero

etch (ECH)—to carve into a hard surface

evolve (eh-VOLV)—to gradually change over time

penalty PEN-uhl-tee—a punishment for breaking the rules

recruit (ri-KROOT)—to encourage someone to join a group or team

rookie (RUH-kee)—a first-year player

replica (REP-leh-kuh)—an exact copy

Zamboni (zam-BONE-ee)—a machine used to resurface ice rinks

READ MORE

Flynn, Brendan. *The History of Hockey*. Minneapolis: Jump!, Inc., 2025.

Gitlin, Marty. *Miracle on Ice*. Ann Arbor, MI: 45th Parallel Press, 2024.

Smith, Elliott. *Hockey's Greatest Myths and Legends*. North Mankato, MN: Capstone, 2023.

INTERNET SITES

Hockey Hall of Fame
hhof.com

Ice Hockey
kids.britannica.com/students/article/ice-hockey/274902

Who Invented Hockey
history.com/news/who-invented-hockey-origins-canada

INDEX

Baker, Hobey, 22, 29
bandy, 7, 10
Bedard, Connor, 18
Brooks, Herb, 21

college hockey, 19, 21, 22, 24, 25
Creighton, James G. A., 8

Darwitz, Natalie, 27

Edwards, Laila, 19

Gathorne-Hardy, Lady Isobel, 9
goalies, 12, 14, 15, 25
Granato, Cammi, 27
Gretzky, Wayne, 16, 17

helmets, 14, 29
Hockey Hall of Fame, 20, 27
Howe, Gordie, 16

Jagr, Jaromir, 23

Knight, Hillary, 19

Lemieux, Mario, 16

McDavid, Connor, 18
Miracle on Ice, 21, 29

National Hockey League (NHL), 9, 11, 12, 13, 14, 16, 18, 20, 21, 23, 25, 28, 29
Native peoples, 7, 10

Olympics, 11, 19, 21, 24, 25, 27, 29
Ovechkin, Alex, 23

pads, 14, 15
Patrick family, 9
Professional Women's Hockey League (PWHL), 26, 28

pucks, 4, 12, 15, 18

records, 17, 20
Rhéaume, Manon, 25
rules, 4, 8, 9, 10, 12, 14

shinny hockey, 10
shinty, 6
skates, 7, 15, 27
Stanley Cup, 9, 20, 21, 29
Stanley, Lord Sir Frederick Arthur, 9, 20, 29

Wickenheiser, Hayley, 27
women's hockey, 19, 24, 25, 26, 27, 29

Zamboni, 11, 29

ABOUT THE AUTHOR

Robb Murray is a journalist and freelance writer who lives in Mankato, Minnesota. He earned a BS degree from Minnesota State University, Mankato. He is married and has two children and one beagle.